The Paisley Rocketeers

by
Donald Malcolm

The 30th Anniversary Committee with the first post war rockets.
Left to right: Peter Stewart with RR-62; Donald Malcolm with RR-65. RR-64 is in the launching rack, while Miss Watson has RR-69 and a test model RR-66. John Stewart holds RR-68 and small test model, RR-63.

© Donald Malcolm 1997
First Published in the United Kingdom, 1997
By Stenlake Publishing, Ochiltree Sawmill, The Lade,
Ochiltree, Ayrshire KA18 2NX
Telephone / fax: 01290 423114

ISBN 1 84033 009 0

To two good friends
Arthur C. Clarke
an early rocketeer,
and
Margaret Morris
who revived the society.

All material and photographs by courtesy of John D. Stewart.

Insignia designed by members for use on their rocket mail.

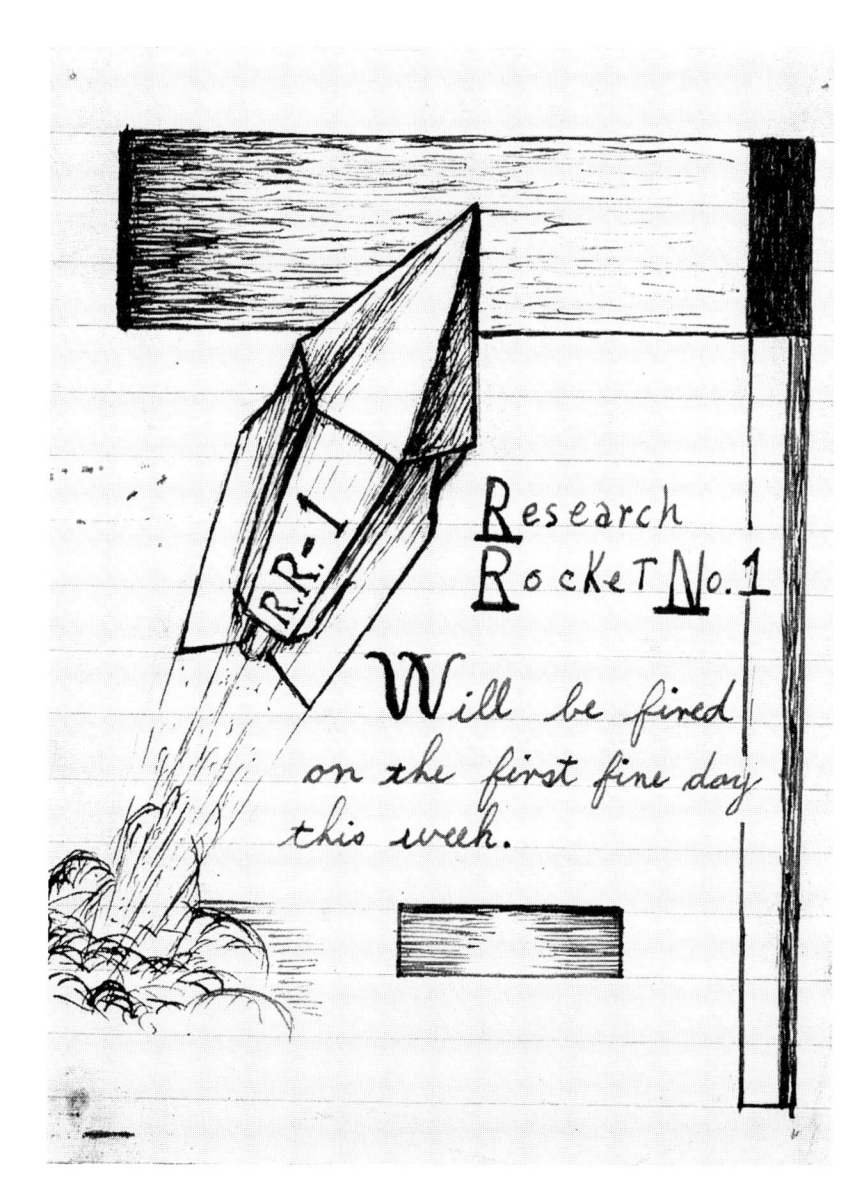

Foreword

1997 is the 40th anniversary of the Space Age. With ever-advancing technology, sustained courage and a vital sense of adventure, men and women have continued to break the ties of Earth, traversing and exploring the vast silences between worlds, and sending probes on endless journeys to the stars.

With the launching of Sputnik I on 4 October 1957 the two superpowers, America and Russia, vied with each other for 'supremacy' in space. Today, the nations co-operate in their space programmes, and while in the early days the crew members were either Russian or American, it is now commonplace to have an Indian, a Japanese, a Cuban or a Briton – the first was Helen Sharman – sharing the duties aboard orbiting space craft.

Among the great pioneers of astronautics were Konstantin Tsiolkovsky (Russia), Robert H. Goddard (USA) and Hermann Oberth (Germany). Probably better-known to the layman is Werner von Braun because of his association with the infamous V-2. His sights had always been set on the peaceful use of rockets and he was the prime architect in the development of the American space programme. Those men laid the scientific and engineering groundwork for all that was to follow from the launch of Sputnik I, a primitive sphere weighing only 183 pounds.

At an amateur level, many people around the world were building model rockets and experimenting with them. Although the hardware of these models was – and is – modest when compared to the giant rockets at Cape Canaveral and Baikonour, the *ideas* behind the work of amateurs in the field have often been very significant. Most amateur rocketeers have no formal qualifications in, say, physics, mathematics or engineering, but their contribution to the field has nonetheless been valuable.

This is the story of one of the world's leading experimenters, John D. Stewart of Paisley, founder of the Paisley Rocketeers Society, still going strong.

Let's go back to 1933 . . .

Donald Malcolm
24 April 1997

The pre-war years

In 1933 John Stewart, a pupil at the prestigious John Neilson Institution in Paisley, was a keen reader of science fiction magazines such as *Air Wonder Stories*. Science fiction had already been around for a long time, although the magazine form of the genre only dated back to 1926, when Hugo Gernsback began to publish *Amazing Stories*. Fired by the vigorously imaginative cover art and stories, John founded a science fiction club in the school in 1933-34 with three or four members.

The British Interplanetary Society (BIS) was also formed in 1933, although use of the word 'interplanetary' represented a leap of faith in a future technology. Most people considered space travel to be a fantasy dreamed up by a group of people who had been reading too much science fiction. At the time the fastest form of travel was by aeroplane. On April 10, piloting a Macchi MC.72 seaplane over Lake Garda, Francesco Agello attained a world record speed of 423 mph. That was over a measured course. The highest rated cruising speed for any commercial machine was 190 mph, achieved by the elegant Heinkel He 70G, which could carry four passengers. Cars and trains were familiar modes of transport, but their speeds were modest in comparison.

Bearing in mind that the required velocities were in *thousands* of miles per hour, it is not surprising that the prospect of travel to the moon and planets by rocket ship was generally ridiculed. Common questions, usually asked with tongue in cheek, were 'what will the rocket push against?', and 'what will prevent it from falling down?' Nonetheless, a couple of years down the road, at Roswell, New Mexico, one of Robert H. Goddard's rockets attained an 'unimaginable' velocity of 700 mph, reaching an altitude of 7,500 feet.

That year, 1935, John Stewart joined the BIS. His receipt was signed by Arthur C. Clarke, who went on to become a trained scientist, the inventor of communications satellites and the world's foremost science fiction writer. He was also one of the early members of the Paisley Rocketeers Society. But I am getting a little ahead of the story.

In the second issue of the BIS *Journal* there was a description of model rocket construction and John's interest was caught. But also printed was a letter from the Home Office stating that no experiments using liquid fuel would be permitted. (In 1926 Goddard had launched the world's first liquid-fuelled rocket, propelled by an oxygen-petrol mixture, at Auburn, Massachusetts.) John sent in a query about rockets to the *Scottish Daily Express*, and some time later an article by a Lord Forbes was printed with some thoughts on rocketry.

His interest in rocket design sparked, John correctly came to the conclusion that an alternative form of propulsion to the propeller was necessary. If flight beyond the atmosphere was contemplated – and it was – then the other means had to be completely independent of the presence of air, essential to the function of a propeller-driven aeroplane. As to what the rocket would push against, Newton's third law of motion provided the answer, stating that 'to every action there is an equal and opposite reaction'.

In 1934 Gerhart Zucker, a German experimenter, visited Scotland and launched a mail-carrying rocket from Scarp, intended to land on Harris. No doubt someone had warned the sheep! His rocket consisted of a five-foot tube with a diameter of about 18", a conical nose and a smaller tube inside to carry the fuel. It had four fins. The event, which took place on the morning of Monday July 28, evidently attracted a mixed audience of the military, civil servants, reporters, Post Office officials and others who were just there, they hoped, to see something blow up – which the rocket duly did. In his account in the *Scots Magazine* of July 1982, John A. Macleod wrote:

'The smoke had cleared. We could see a tangle of wood and iron: a beach strewn with letters, some of them smouldering, with people running around stamping on the little fires and salvaging the mail; a disconsolate Herr Zucker with his head in his hands.'

Down the ages, inventors have tended to do a lot of that.

Zucker's second experiment took place in the South of England, but the flight was erratic and only partially successful; disconsolate, he returned to Germany.

In October 1935, John Stewart made a plan for a projectile based around seven firework-type rockets, bought at a penny each from Annie Howatt, who had a confectioner shop in Caledonia Street, Paisley (the shop was more like a Jennie A' Things, for she sold much more than just sweeties). The total weight of the rockets, along with the mail that was attached to them, was two and a half ounces. John has kept a record of all his activities since 1935, including a lively account of the event at Underwood Road, Paisley, near to the Post Office Sorting Depot (see page 9).

That episode showed just how dangerous even a small rocket can be. Anyone who has seen archive footage of American experiments with captured V-2s, or catastrophes on a much larger scale at Cape Canaveral, will realise why ground-based personnel kept well clear of the launch pad.

Maybe Shakespeare was watching the Globe Theatre fall down for the second or third time when he thought of his phrase, 'There's a destiny shapes our ends, rough-hew them how we may'. If experiments always succeeded first time and there was no head-holding, then life would be a dull affair. When I was taking notes for this book, John told me that, had Research Rocket No.1 been a success, then he might not have been stimulated to find, by further experiment, what went wrong and how it could be rectified.

As recorded in the *Model Rocketeer*, March 1983, John recalled that '. . . while James Cunningham, who was studying chemistry, prepared some reports on solid fuels, our main research was in aerodynamic and other aspects of rocketry such as stabilising methods, recovery systems, payload carrying, staging, performance improvements, aerial photography, rocket planes, and so on.' Ideas, not just hardware.

Several more experiments followed RR-1, with varying degrees of success. RR-5 was the first large model, built around a four-ounce rocket tube and carrying a parachute. The launch took place at the school sports field at Ferguslie – then just fields – and the vertical ascent appeared to be going well when the parachute blew out and the rocket crashed. RR-8 was no more fortunate. It took off at an angle and was immediately caught by the following wind, after which it struck the ground and went 'bouncing across the field, hissing and sparking, and scattering mail, parachute, and broken sticks in its wake'.

RR-9 was an important model. One of the three rocket tubes positioned around a thin stick was slightly advanced to ensure the ignition of the other two, a clever solution to the problem of mis-fires. It was a soaring success, zipping over the tenements at Underwood Road and landing on the road, near to the present site of the sorting office. That was on 25 February 1936. The experimenters met at John's house after the flight and discussions culminated in the decision to form a rocket society. That was the unanimous verdict of those present: James Cunningham, Quintin Baillie, Charles Kay, Wallace McKellar, Grahame Paul, John Stewart and his brother Peter. John duly drew up a constitution and on the 27th the Paisley Rocketeers was officially founded. A New Constitution of 1938 permitted non-local members to join, among them Arthur C. Clarke and Eric Burgess, who had founded two organisations, the Manchester Interplanetary Society in July 1936 and the Manchester Astronautical Association in December 1937.

Up until the outbreak of World War Two, the society embarked on a series of experimental flights. John extended his Book of Reports, in which he recorded his own experiments, to include details of rockets built by other members. The oldest member of the group, chemistry student James Cunningham, was given the grand-sounding title of Chemical Research Chief. This was not as risible as it seems; James worked in the chemistry department of Brown and Polson and can have been no more than twenty-one when he went to war, only to be captured at Dunkirk. He used his time as a POW to study for, and gain, his BSc. Eventually he became Chief Research Officer for the Morgan Crucible Company of Cardiff, which was engaged on rocket research.

With the Rocketeers, James investigated and reported on the suitability of various fuels for use in rockets, although experiments with liquid fuels were confined to HM Forces by the Home Office. If citizens were going to get blown up, then it had to be done officially. More serious accidents could be hidden under the aegis of the fifty-year rule and with luck, no one would notice anything amiss.

But such restrictions didn't prevent James from developing his own ideas, and one that was surely prescient was the concept of a rocket fuel in paste form which could be squeezed into tubes and left to harden. Apparently Polaris rockets were filled by a similar process. As John notes, this avoided 'the dangerous ramming of the powder normally used in firework rockets'.

Societies of all kinds produce publications and the PRS was no exception. The first issue of their magazine consisted of eight typed pages, and members received the single copy in turn. That was in March 1936. Two more 'Paisley Rocketeers Reports' were circulated in June and September. In February a professionally duplicated four page magazine called 'The Rocket' was produced, followed by further issues in March and June. Two years of the Society's research and other activities, 1936-38, was summarised in 'Conclusions', published in March 1938.

But the first brief phase of the existence of the Paisley Rocketeers Society was soon to come to a close. Hitler was causing trouble in the Sudetenland, Czechoslovakia – 'a small country, far away' – and all too soon real rockets would be devastating cities such as Antwerp and London.

A not so gentle let-down

The Paisley Rocketeers weren't firing off rockets just for the fun of it, although there was always a large element of that. Each launching had an objective in mind. The mid-air release of a small container of mail was accomplished by RR-16 on 14 May 1936. The carrier rocket sizzled skywards from behind the John Neilson at Oakshaw, and all went well until the parachute detached from the rocket at a height of about 195 feet. The parachute was too large, so that the comparatively light load of mail had no effect on it and the experimenters could only watch helplessly as it drifted towards the observatory, never to be found. Perhaps someone decided to keep a souvenir from the skies as proof of an early, 'X Files'-type visitation. The rocket itself dug a small hole down the brae and achieved the status of a relic of an experiment slightly gone wrong. But that's the nature of experimentation and the Rocketeers were not discouraged.

And to prove that persistence pays off, RR-20, launched in June, was an unqualified success. The designer learned from experience and the rocket had two parachutes, the smaller one for the mail, the larger to soft-land the rocket. The skies above Ferguslie reverberated to a gentle roar as it thrust upwards for about 325 feet, the ends of the long card fins being ripped off by its rapid passage. As it reached its maximum altitude and began to head back to the ground, both parachutes were released and the experimenters had the deserved satisfaction of retrieving the rocket and payload when they landed. RR-20's success was duly reported in *The Neilson News* of 12 June 1936.

On 15 December a Model Rocket Contest was held by enthusiastic members at Oakshaw Brae. Each entrant was given a free rocket tube, around which they built their rockets, so that all contestants would be using the same type. Eight of the ten applicants flew their rockets. The resulting flights mixed success and failure and the winner was Roy Wilson with a down-range distance of about 400 ft. That was probably the world's first rocket contest.

1937 got off to a flying start, when RR-32 took the long distance record for a quarter ounce rocket tube to about 580 feet. The purpose of the flight was to test a new shape of thrust augmentor. Rockets fly most efficiently when the speed of the rocket equals the speed of the exhaust, and the thrust augmentor was designed to help improve this balance. The rocket, which was launched from the south-west corner of the John Neilson, crashed in Underwood Lane – and was promptly crushed by a passing vehicle. It was just as well that they didn't collide; think of the insurance implications!

The site of the next experiment was at Tarbert, Loch Fyne, where RR-40, the last pre-war model to carry any mail, was launched on 16 August. John hoped that the rocket would traverse the neck of the loch, but defeated by the distance it parachuted in the sea. The equivalent of America's space recovery naval task force was John's father and brother in a rowing boat. They managed to salvage the rocket, but three of the four letters aboard had drifted away and were lost.

Rocket-tube ejection was one of the ongoing experiments in 1937.

The idea was to try and reduce the impact damage of smaller models by dispensing with the weight of a parachute – remember, any additional weight has an effect on performance. Two models were successful in reducing weight by the automatic ejection in flight of the spent rocket-tube, but loss of momentum meant that shorter ranges were achieved.

1937 finished on a spectacular note with the launch of what is probably the world's first successful three-stage rocket. The principle of the rocket is the one that put Yuri Gagarin in space in 1961 and carried the crew of Apollo Eleven to the first moon landing. The payload of a rocket is always a very small proportion of the all-up weight (the weight of the rocket that launched Sputnik 1 was 105,000 lbs; the satellite weighed only 183 lbs) and the trick is to obtain the maximum efficiency from the fuel carried. A single-stage rocket that could carry enough fuel to take a man into an orbit 100 miles above the earth wouldn't get off the launch pad. Instead, fuel is carried in three stages, the largest one doing the donkey work of launching the rocket. After lift-off has been achieved, and the fuel of the first stage has been exhausted, it is dead weight. So, having imparted its momentum to the second and third stages, it is detached. The procedure is repeated with the second stage and finally the last stage builds up the velocity necessary to place the capsule in orbit. The first attributed design was by Conrad Haas (1529-69), Chief of the Artillery Arsenal at Sibiu, Romania.

The RR-47 launch took place at St James' Park, Paisley, on 31 December 1937. The rocket, which weighed two-and-a-quarter ounces, probably travelled down-range about 1,000 feet; the second stage landed about 800 feet away. The third stage was never recovered and when the model was presented to the Museum of Childhood at Edinburgh, a replacement was provided.

1938 and 1939 were quiet years for the Rocketeers. The highlight was what might have been the world's first attempt at aerial photography from a rocket. The experiment took place at Tarbert, Loch Fyne, on 22 August 1938 and though the rocket soared high above the castle John recalled ruefully that it 'decided instead to photograph the blue Tarbert sky'.

Other experiments were made with spin-stabilised models (rockets with no stick or fins), an extended expansion nozzle, and a means of igniting the rocket-tube centrally to improve the flow of the exhaust gases.

With the outbreak of war, the Paisley Rocketeers Society was dissolved and the first, eventful phase of its existence was over.

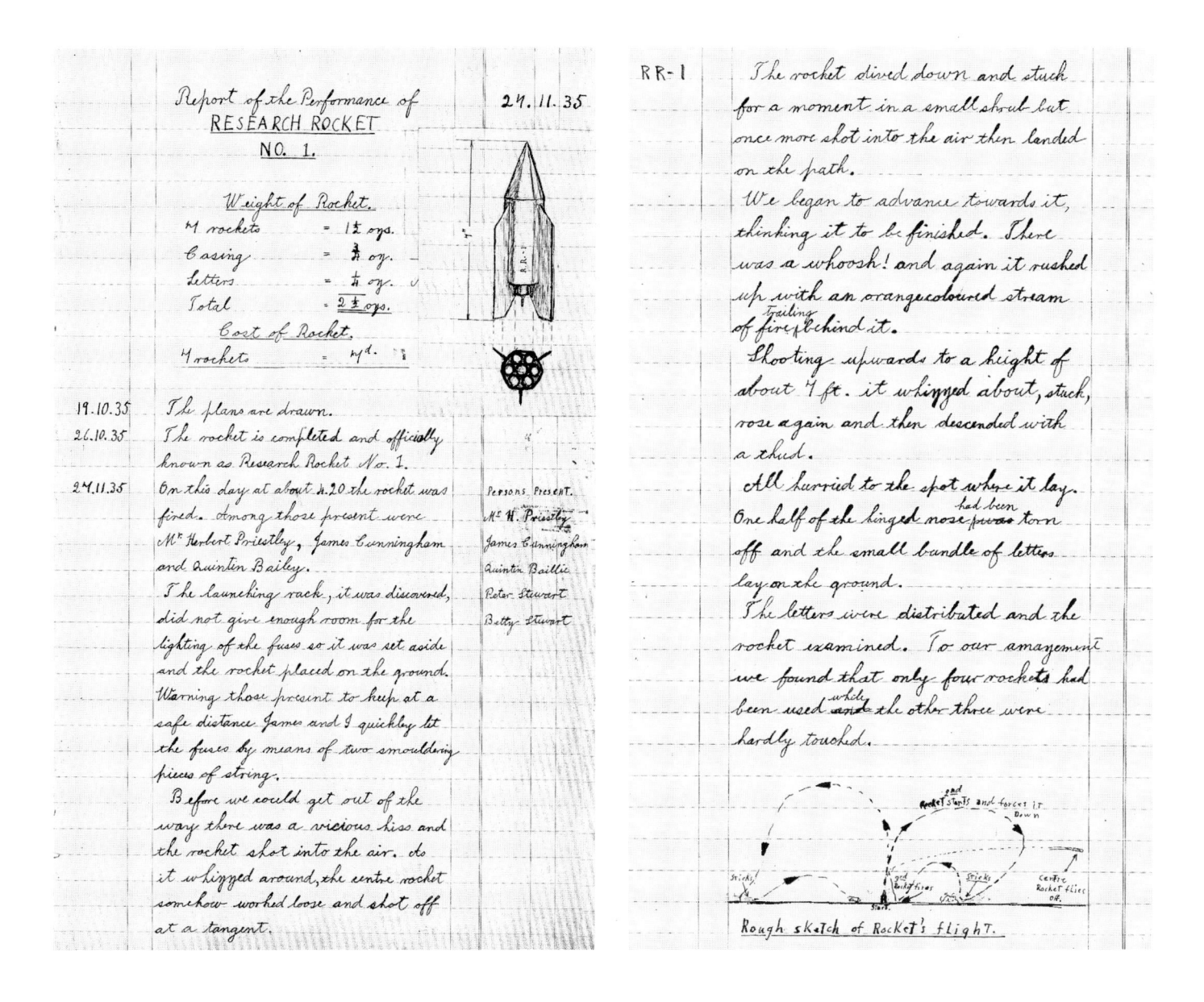

Report of the Performance of
RESEARCH ROCKET NO. 1.

24.11.35

Weight of Rocket.
7 rockets	= 1½ ozs.
Casing	= ¾ oz.
Letters	= ¼ oz.
Total	= 2½ ozs.

Cost of Rocket.
7 rockets = 7d.

19.10.35	The plans are drawn.
26.10.35	The rocket is completed and officially known as Research Rocket No. 1.
24.11.35	On this day at about 4.20 the rocket was fired. Among those present were Mr Herbert Priestley, James Cunningham and Quintin Bailey.

The launching rack, it was discovered, did not give enough room for the lighting of the fuses so it was set aside and the rocket placed on the ground. Warning those present to keep at a safe distance James and I quickly lit the fuses by means of two smouldering pieces of string.

Before we could get out of the way there was a vicious hiss and the rocket shot into the air. As it whipped around, the centre rocket somehow worked loose and shot off at a tangent.

Persons Present.
Mr H. Priestley
James Cunningham
Quintin Baillie
Peter Stewart
Betty Stewart

RR-1

The rocket dived down and stuck for a moment in a small shrub but once more shot into the air then landed on the path.

We began to advance towards it, thinking it to be finished. There was a whoosh! and again it rushed up with an orange coloured stream of fire trailing behind it.

Shooting upwards to a height of about 7 ft. it whipped about, stuck, rose again and then descended with a thud.

All hurried to the spot where it lay. One half of the hinged nose had been torn off and the small bundle of letters lay on the ground.

The letters were distributed and the rocket examined. To our amazement we found that only four rockets had been used while the other three were hardly touched.

Rough sketch of Rocket's flight.

The group prior to the firing of three rockets on 19 May 1936. James Cunningham took the picture, with John Stewart at the back, Quintin Baillie and Peter Stewart on the left, and Willie McGarroch and David Baille to the right. The rockets are (left to right) two-stage MR-10 by Q. Baillie; a near duplicate of RR-15; and MR-9 by D. Baillie.

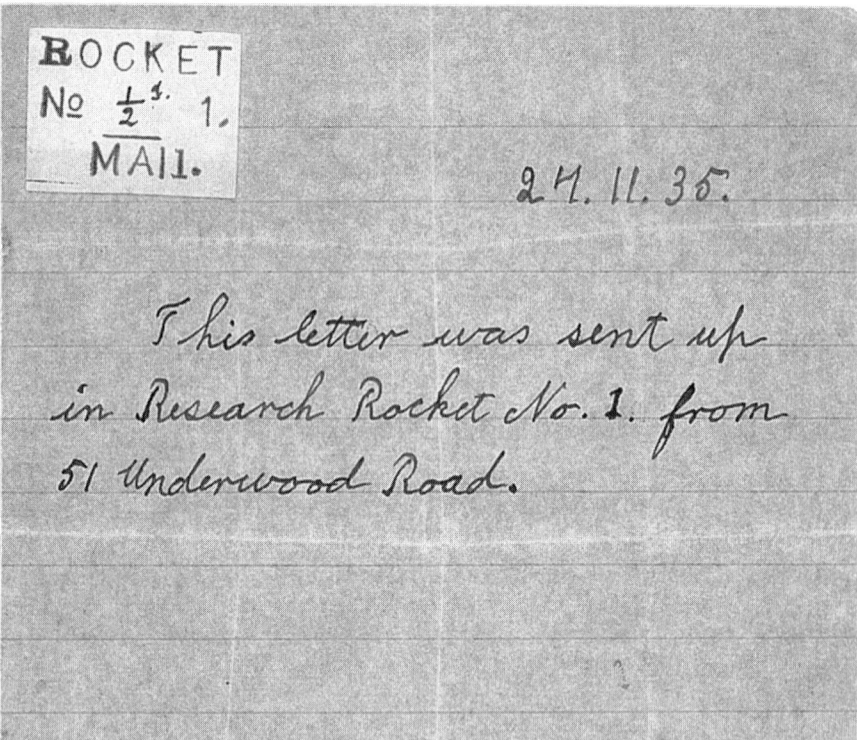

> ROCKET No ½ 1. MAIL.
>
> 24. 11. 35.
>
> This letter was sent up in Research Rocket No. 1. from 51 Underwood Road.

It was originally intended that RR-1 should have a parachute, but when this idea was abandoned it was decided to fly mail in the rocket instead. Six sheets like this were prepared with six 'stamps'. No cancellation was used, nor was there any inscription on the other five. Early items of rocket mail such as this are now highly sought after by philatelists. Unfortunately, the six letters carried in RR-1 were sold to people who had subsequently died or mislaid them when, years later, we tried to trace the letters. This one was purchased by John Stewart's aunt, who gave him a silver 3d piece for it. It was found by his mother when she was dusting the contents of a large bookcase. His aunt had been using it as a bookmark!

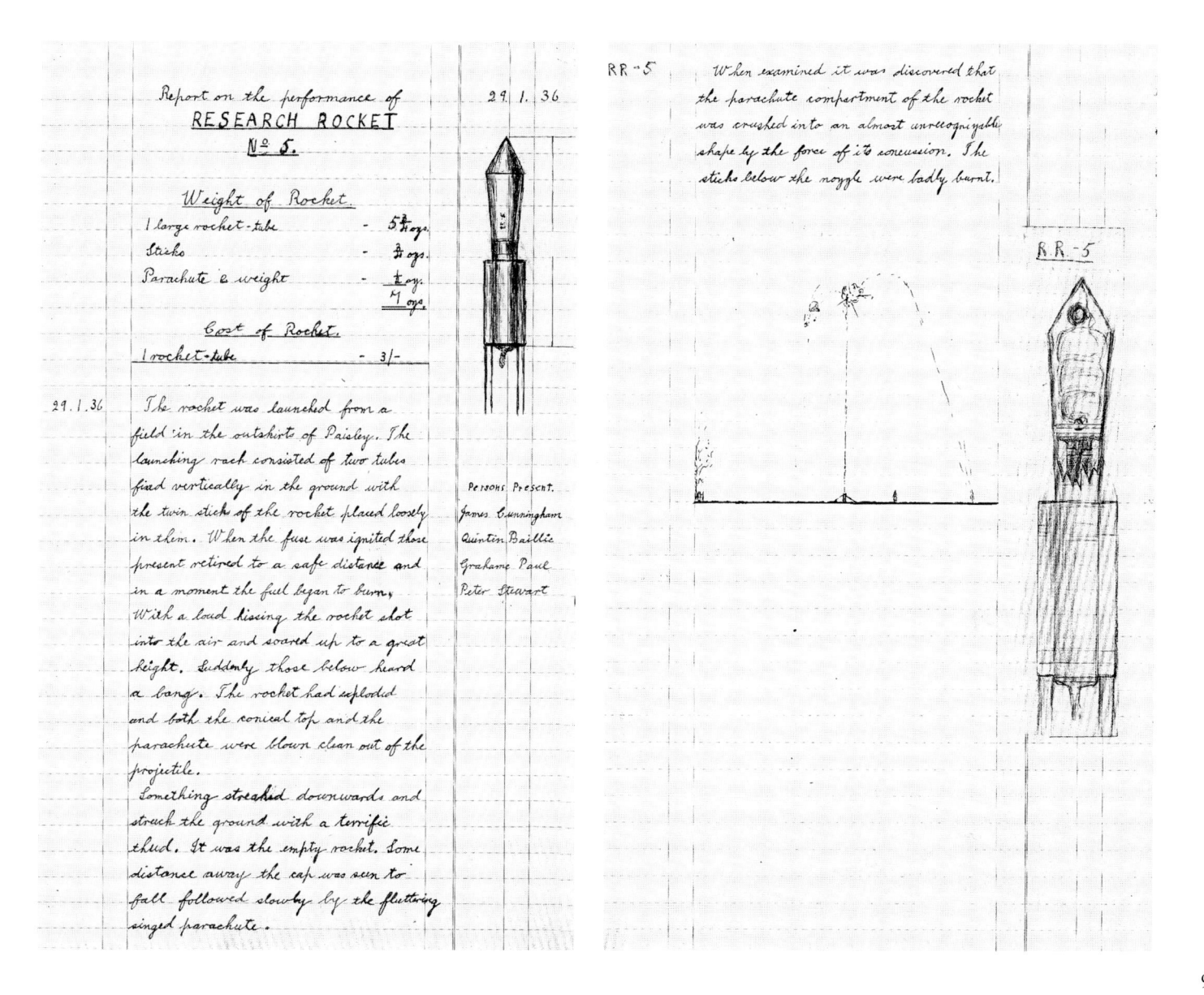

Report on the performance of
RESEARCH ROCKET
№ 5.

29.1.36

Weight of Rocket.
1 large rocket-tube	-	5¾ ozs.
Sticks	-	¾ ozs.
Parachute & weight	-	½ oz.
		7 ozs.

Cost of Rocket.
1 rocket-tube — 3/-

29.1.36 The rocket was launched from a field in the outskirts of Paisley. The launching rack consisted of two tubes fixed vertically in the ground with the twin sticks of the rocket placed loosely in them. When the fuse was ignited those present retired to a safe distance and in a moment the fuel began to burn. With a loud hissing the rocket shot into the air and soared up to a great height. Suddenly those below heard a bang. The rocket had exploded and both the conical top and the parachute were blown clean out of the projectile.

Something streaked downwards and struck the ground with a terrific thud. It was the empty rocket. Some distance away the cap was seen to fall followed slowly by the fluttering singed parachute.

Persons Present.
James Cunningham
Quintin Baillie
Grahame Paul
Peter Stewart

RR-5 When examined it was discovered that the parachute compartment of the rocket was crushed into an almost unrecognisable shape by the force of its concussion. The sticks below the nozzle were badly burnt.

RR-5

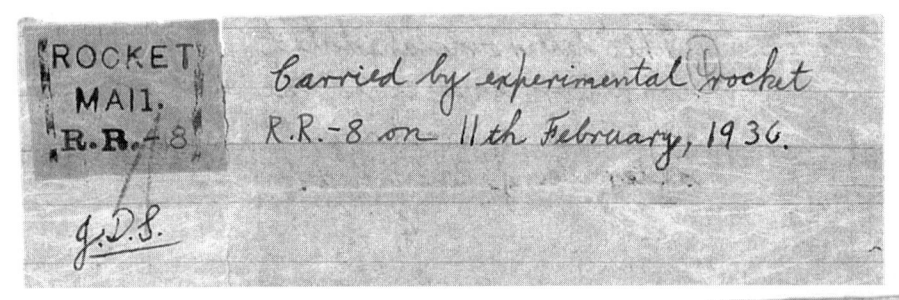

Some more examples of early rocket mail. So far as we remember, eight or ten letters, with stamp, were prepared for launching in RR-8. The mail was placed in a small, round cardboard box, with parachute, which was to be ejected in flight. Only six of the letters would fit in the box, and an inverted 'V' cancellation was used to identify those that had been flown.

One of the unflown letters for RR-8 was flown in RR-14. The inscription was by Mrs Kate Stewart. RR-14's rocket tube could be replaced for second and third firings.

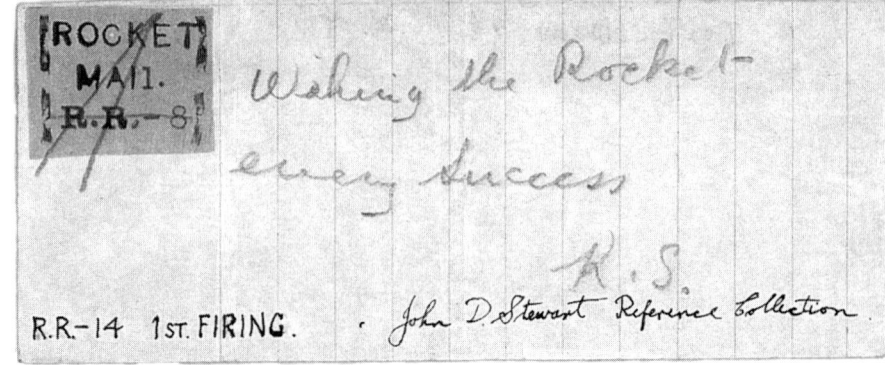

Only four of the six letters, this time with typed stamp, could be accommodated in the round cardboard box, with parachute, which was ejected from RR-20 in flight.

10

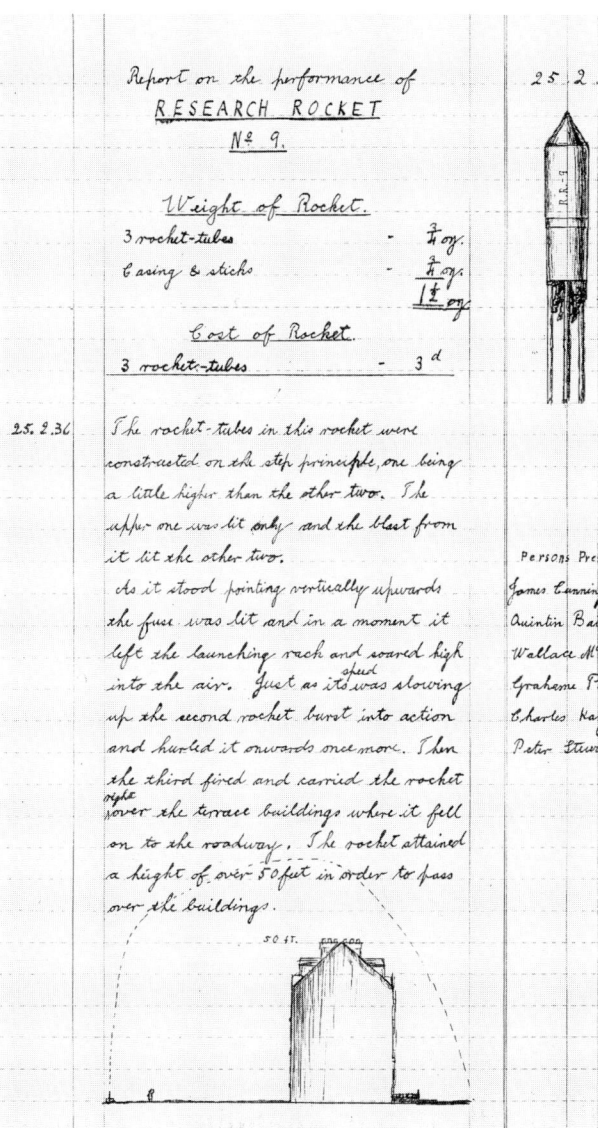

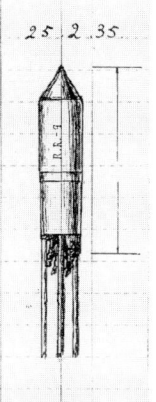

Report on the performance of
RESEARCH ROCKET
N⁰ 9.

25.2.35.

Weight of Rocket.
3 rocket-tubes — ¾ oz.
Casing & sticks — ½ oz.
                    1¼ oz.

Cost of Rocket.
3 rocket-tubes — 3d

25.2.36

The rocket-tubes in this rocket were constructed on the step principle, one being a little higher than the other two. The upper one was lit only and the blast from it lit the other two.

As it stood pointing vertically upwards the fuse was lit and in a moment it left the launching rack and soared high into the air. Just as it's speed was slowing up the second rocket burst into action and hurled it onwards once more. Then the third fired and carried the rocket right over the terrace buildings where it fell on to the roadway. The rocket attained a height of over 50 feet in order to pass over the buildings.

Persons Present.
James Cunningham
Quintin Baillie
Wallace McKellar
Grahame Paul
Charles Kay
Peter Stewart

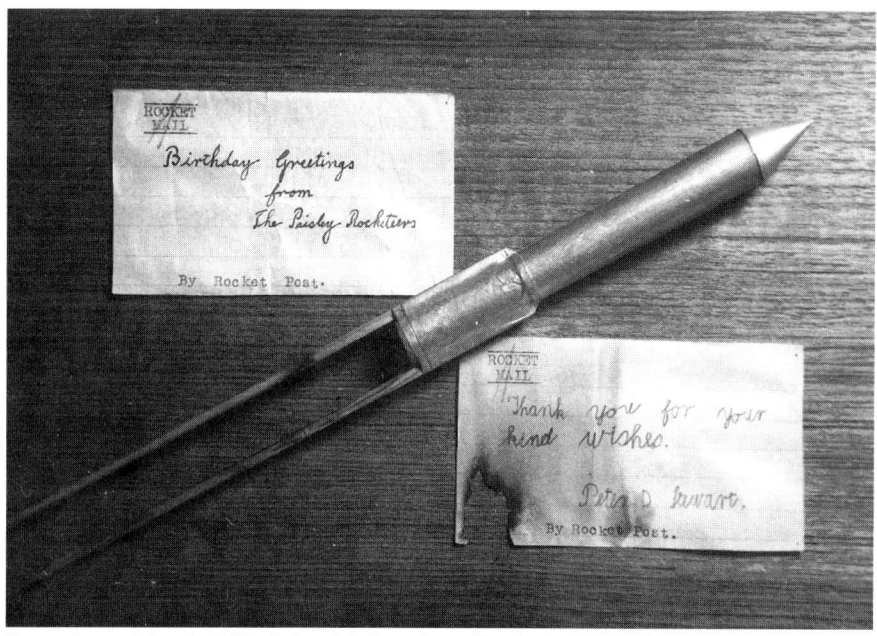

One of two identical Birthday Mail rockets fired on 14 April 1936 along the back gardens at Underwood Road. The first travelled 250 feet and the second 180, against the wind. The burn was caused by the leakage of hot gases through the cork plug at the top of the motor (rocket tube). When Peter received the greetings message he wrote the reply, placed it in the second rocket, and launched it back to the members at No. 51.

After RR-9's successful flight the experimenters met at John Stewart's house and unanimously decided to form a rocket society.

11

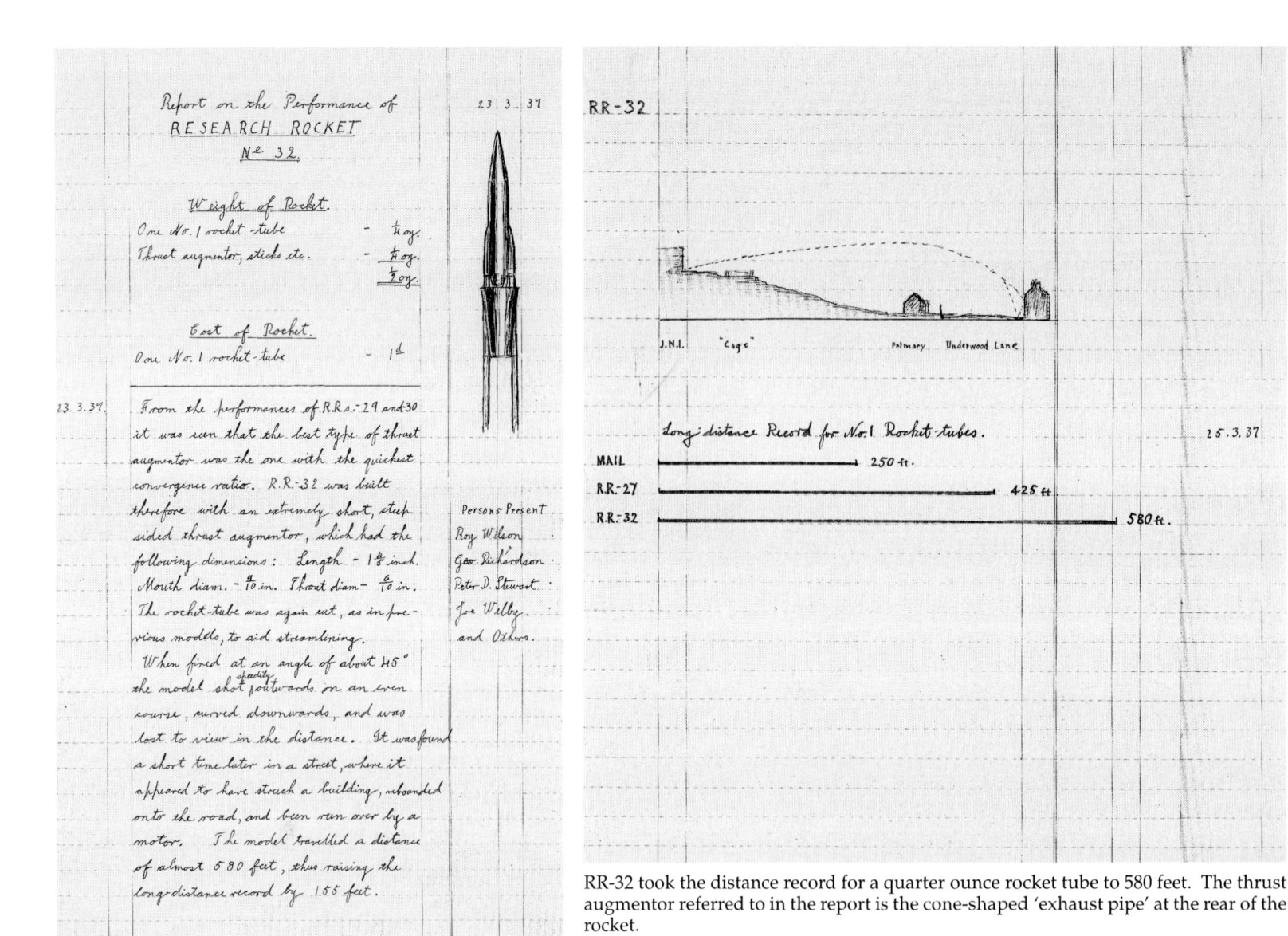

Report on the Performance of
RESEARCH ROCKET
Nº. 32.

23.3.37

Weight of Rocket.
One No. 1 rocket-tube — ¼ oz.
Thrust augmentor, sticks etc. — ¼ oz.
— ½ oz.

Cost of Rocket.
One No. 1 rocket-tube — 1d.

23.3.37 From the performances of R.R.s.- 29 and 30 it was seen that the best type of thrust augmentor was the one with the quickest convergence ratio. R.R.-32 was built therefore with an extremely short, steep sided thrust augmentor, which had the following dimensions: Length - 1½ inch. Mouth diam.- 9/10 in. Throat diam- 6/10 in. The rocket-tube was again cut, as in previous models, to aid streamlining.
When fired at an angle of about 45° the model shot sharply outwards on an even course, curved downwards, and was lost to view in the distance. It was found a short time later in a street, where it appeared to have struck a building, rebounded onto the road, and been run over by a motor. The model travelled a distance of almost 580 feet, thus raising the long-distance record by 155 feet.

Persons Present
Roy Wilson
Geo. Richardson
Peter D. Stewart
Joe Welby.
and Others.

RR-32

J.N.I.   "Cage"   Primary   Underwood Lane

Long distance Record for No. 1 Rocket-tubes.   25.3.37
MAIL —————— 250 ft.
R.R.-27 ————————— 425 ft.
R.R.-32 ————————————— 580 ft.

RR-32 took the distance record for a quarter ounce rocket tube to 580 feet. The thrust augmentor referred to in the report is the cone-shaped 'exhaust pipe' at the rear of the rocket.

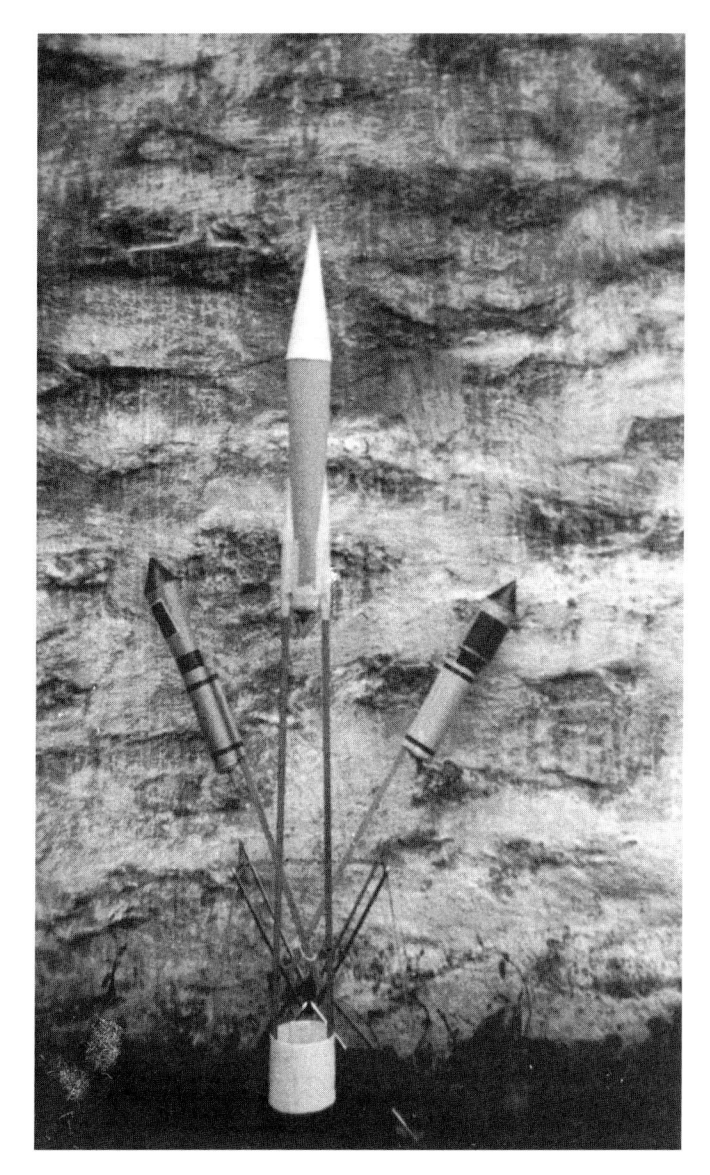

RR-40 flanked by two unadulterated skyrocket 'motors'. The ring of paper at the back of the rocket is the stability tube, a device designed to help maintain a straight flight path. It was hoped that RR-40 would bridge the narrow neck of East Loch Tarbert, but one side of the stability tube bent inwards, holding it back, and it parachuted into the sea. Four hand-drawn pieces of mail were carried, two in the nosecone, which was lost, and two tucked into the stability tube. Only the letter in the side of the stability tube which bent inwards was recovered, the other had floated out.

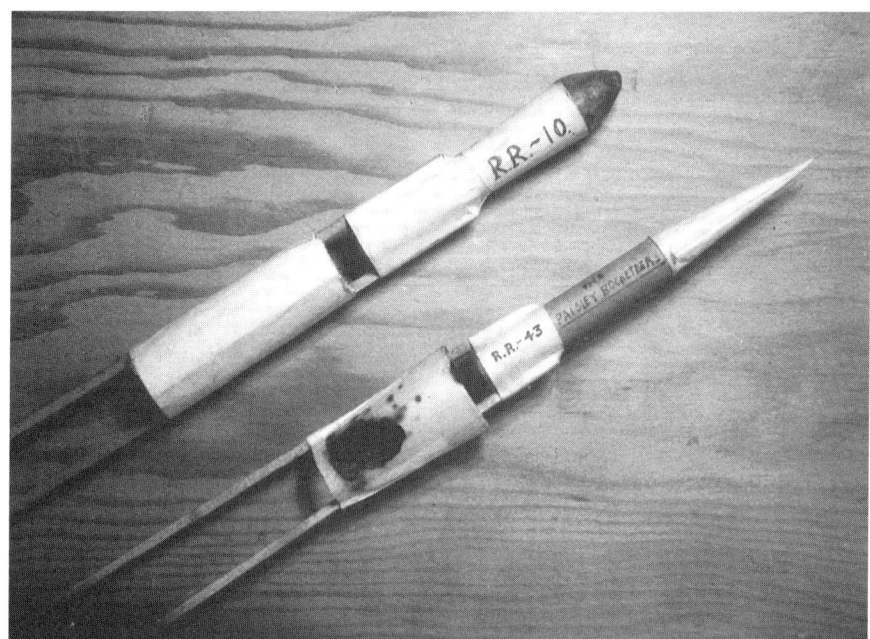

RR-10 and RR-43. The latter was similar to record-breaking RR-32 (which broke distance records for its type), but had a more steeply converging thrust augmentor. This burnt through at one side at the second launching, but the rocket still travelled 400 feet.

Betty Stewart with the first photographic rocket, RR-53, just before launch. The camera lens can be seen, central in the upper half of the rocket, with the launch tube in the foreground. After taking a picture, the rocket drifted on its parachute for about 600 feet and landed, upright, in marshy ground at the far side of Tarbert Castle. 22 August 1938.

Peter Stewart with the second camera rocket, RR-55. A small mirror at 45° reflected what was behind the rocket into the camera lens. It was underpowered, however, and the parachute ripped as the model fell to earth. No photo was obtained. This picture was taken at the bandstand on the east side of St James' Park.

John Stewart with three large pyrotechnic rockets. Commercially-produced firework rockets such as these acted as 'motors' for the rocketeers' more technologically sophisticated models, which were built around them. The sticks for these rockets have been cut to half size for ease of transport.

The Rocketeers rediscovered

During discussions, John reminded me that I had rediscovered the Paisley Rocketeers, something that I had forgotten. I had come across reference to the pre-war experimenters when I was gathering information for what was to be my first published work, an article entitled 'Dawn of the Space Age' which appeared in the *Paisley Daily Express* in August 1955. Someone passed on my request for information to John, who was working in London at the time, and we eventually met up.

However, the re-constitution of the Society did not occur until 1965 and Mrs Margaret Morris (nee Watson), philatelist of international repute, is credited with the revival. She purchased a collection of rocket mail and photographs from the early activities, 1936-39, and I was able to put her in touch with John, who authenticated the material.

During a meeting, Margaret pointed out that the coming November would be the 30th anniversary of the firing of RR-1 and suggested that a special cover be produced to mark the occasion. John thought that the interest in small pre-war rockets would be minimal, given the great achievements in space since 1957, but our persuasive arguments carried the day. John designed and arranged the printing of a special cover, I designed a special cachet and handled the sales, and when John suggested that he design a rocket to fly some of the mail – which he did – Margaret agreed to hand-letter the addresses on those covers. John's brother, Peter, was co-opted on to the PRS 30th anniversary committee and we were in business.

RR-62 was launched from the top of the Gleniffer Braes, opposite the car park at Robertson Park on 27 November 1965. The model was overloaded and made only a brief flight, plunging in deep snow before the parachute had a chance to deploy.

On the 30th anniversary of the founding of the original Paisley Rocketeers Society, 27 February 1966, a special cover was produced and 54 copies flown in three rockets from the quarry above Glen Park, courtesy of Mr Lamont of Brownside Farm.

As a result of these renewed activities, connections were being made around the world. Midlands groups were formed, taking their cue from Paisley. Perry F. Zwisler, of Massachusetts, decided to include the pre-war PRS mail in an international catalogue of rocket mail, then nearing its completion. All the committee members received a beautiful book and a set of rocket mail covers, from Mr O. K. Rumbel.

John wished to repay this generosity and to strengthen the links between two rocket groups. O.K. Rumbel and his son Keith, of Mission, Texas, had flown the 'First International Rocket Mail' over the Rio Grande from America to Mexico and back again on 2 July 1936. John conceived the idea of producing the 'First Transatlantic Rocket Mail' – by firing rockets across the narrow stretch of the sea at Clachan Bridge, near Oban. It is sometimes called 'the only bridge over the Atlantic'. John designed two manuscript greetings which, with 75 copies, were flown in three rockets at Clachan on 2 July 1966. At the time, the Rumbels were publishing a booklet celebrating their own anniversary flights and the greetings were reproduced in it.

About this time, Margaret discovered that there was a new type of model rocket on sale, propelled by water and compressed air. John started to experiment with his own water-propelled rockets. The commercial model was potentially dangerous, pressurised by a hand-held pump and requiring the number of pump strokes to be counted. John's solution was to design a launching rack that could be stuck in the ground and connected to a long length of tubing. This was attached to a car pump with a gauge, and provided a much safer and more efficient method of preparing the rockets. John coined the term 'aquajet' for water-propelled models. Many experiments have been carried out since then and improvements made in design and performance.

Many Paisley Buddies will have cause to remember the hurricane of January 1968. (I went out one morning to find the garden hut scattered around in pieces. As it had been barely standing together in pieces, things weren't as bad as they might have been.) The Provost set up a storm relief fund and John flew special covers in aid of it. The mail carried the proudly revived title of the Paisley Rocketeers Society, which was formally reconstituted on 23 February 1968. The aim was to foster the development of small rockets for peaceful purposes. It made a welcome change from the weight of military hardware then threatening the world, and charity flights were to feature strongly in future experiments.

In all 100 charity covers were flown in aquajet A-16. Load one (1-50) was flown twice into Loch Lomond, at Balloch; load two (51-100) made three flights. After each splash-down, the rocket was recovered from a boat by Peter Stewart and Alexander Lochhead. Some covers were slightly damaged by water leakage.

The Scottish National Institution for War Blinded was next to benefit from a charity flight, held at the Linburn Estate, Edinburgh. 100 Paisley Pattern covers were carried. Both BBC TV and ITV Scottish news featured the event that evening. *The Scotsman* ran a photograph – and someone with nothing better to do reported it to HM Inspector of Explosives. His fuse was lit at the wrong end, for he immediately assumed that the PRS was manufacturing rockets. What ensued merely goes to prove how silly and obtrusive bureaucrats can be.

In July 1969 the Society received a letter from the Home Office. The inspector quoted the Explosives Act of 1875, stating '. . . any process of such manufacture shall not be carried out except in a factory licensed by the Secretary of State for the purpose'. The PRS replied that there was no desire, or intention, to make propellant and load it into rocket-tubes. Instead, commercially available tubes were used, and interest lay mainly in the aerodynamic factors affecting rocket flight. The Home Office remained obtuse: 'I have considered the points you raise in your letter, but I remain of the opinion that putting a propellant charge, or rocket-tube into a rocket in these circumstances is dangerous and illegal . . .'.

The Rocketeers fired another salvo. 'We are perturbed that you regard the putting of a *rocket-tube* into a model rocket as "dangerous and illegal", and must confess that we cannot see in what special respect doing this differs from, say, the insertion of a blank cartridge into a gun, or the filling with petrol of a car, or a cigarette lighter. These latter operations we consider more dangerous. However, we can confirm that our use of the rocket-tube was suspended on receipt of [your] letter of 8th July.'

This failed to satisfy the bureaucrats, however, and the inspectorate stuck to their opinion.

'Manufacture' is the significant word in the interpretation of the Act of 1875. As the PRS pointed out, it means 'regular production, usually for sale'. The society's model-making depended on art or craft and the experimental detail tended to differ with each rocket built.

It had been intended to celebrate the 50th anniversary of the first double-crossing of the Atlantic in 1919 by the R-34 airship, built by Beardmore at Inchinnan. A rocket contest with the participation of the Midland Rocket Association, making a trip to Paisley, was cancelled, although aquajet A-19 carried commemorative mail to mark the event.

Incredulous as it might seem, the Home Office had yet another shot in its locker (propelled by a standard-issue elastic band, no doubt). In August 1969, HM Inspector of Explosives wrote 'We have always regarded fuelling a rocket by any means 'manufacture' in this sense, and therefore illegal unless licensed: thus the same objections would apply to your fuelling the rockets in other ways, now that the use of rocket-tubes has been discontinued.'

The use of aquajets was suspended and legal advice sought. One adviser amusingly summed up the pompous reaction of the Home Office by saying 'If your aquajets come under the Explosives Act, then you will soon require a gun license for a water pistol'. There was no breach of the law and the PRS continued to use aquajets.

The Paisley Rocketeers Society continued to experiment, and still does. A phenomenon known as 'spin-glide' was noted in three flights of MA-18. An aquajet with fins normally heads nose-first for the ground, but MA-18 was observed to go into a near-horizontal spin-glide. The model achieved prolonged flights and made bounce landings, one of which took the aquajet to about 350 feet.

A number of aquajet contests have been held. The third was specially staged for Dave Allen and a television team in 1976 and the *Express* of 24 June printed a feature headed 'Sixteen Rocket Salute for Dave Allen'. The comedian and his team were at the contest for about four hours and part of the recording was screened nation-wide in the 'Dave Allen and Friends' series in spring 1977.

Flights have taken place at Oban, Edinburgh, Loch Lomond, Dunoon, Innellan, Largs, over Erskine and the Clyde and at Hill House, Helensburgh. And no doubt there will be more flights as we approach 2001 (the true Millenium date). That just happens to be the 65th anniversary of the founding of the Paisley Rocketeers Society.

The 30th anniversary of RR-1. Donald and Gordon Malcolm, Peter Stewart, and Dr A.E. Roy look on as John Stewart prepares RR-62 for launch on the snow-covered Gleniffer Braes, 27 November 1965.

RR-62 blasts out of the launching rack. The lift-off was quite fast and noisy, but a stiff south-westerly breeze coming over the hill probably contributed to the model's instability, and it curved over to strike the snow-covered grass barely 150 feet from the launch site. The parachute was ejected on the ground.

John and Peter Stewart examine the rocket after its flight. The nosecone was not crushed so it must have made a near-horizontal landing. The mail was neither wet nor scorched when removed later for posting on the same day.

Celebrating the 30th anniversary of the foundation of the Paisley Rocketeers. The launching party had an international flavour with left to right: J.K. Leung, a student from Hong Kong; Bill Drennen on a visit from Wilmington, USA; Peter Stewart and young Peter; Margaret Watson; John Stewart and Donald Malcolm. Three rockets were launched. The first (above) was RR-62, containing a further fourteen covers commemorating RR-1. Second was RR-64 with twenty PRS anniversary covers, and, thirdly, RR-65 also with twenty PRS covers. The site was on Brownside Braes, about one-and-three-quarter miles east of the previous site. Potterhill can be seen behind the trees of Glen Park, with *Thorscraig* at the right.

Peter and John Stewart making final adjustments to the launching rack. This incorporated springs to catapult the rocket into the sky, augmenting the power of the rocket. The catapult worked perfectly for all three launches.

Lift off of RR-62 (second flight). The stiff north-east wind has already blown the first smoke to one side. (A normal south-west wind would have been much more favourable).

ROCKETS GALORE

THE SAGA OF THE PAISLEY ROCKETEERS

A heading prepared by John Stewart for Donald Malcolm's short history of the Rocketeers in the *Paisley Daily Express* of 5 March 1966. The model space ship was for use in an over-ambitious film which was never completed. Peter Stewart is the spectator.

The printer had made a fine job of the 30th anniversary covers, and the problem was how to fly twenty of them without damage. We decided that binding them around a stability tube would be the best solution. Layers of wrinkled foil prevented any scorching; the thicker layer of foil which gave protection on the outside was later cut into small flown labels to meet the demand for souvenirs.

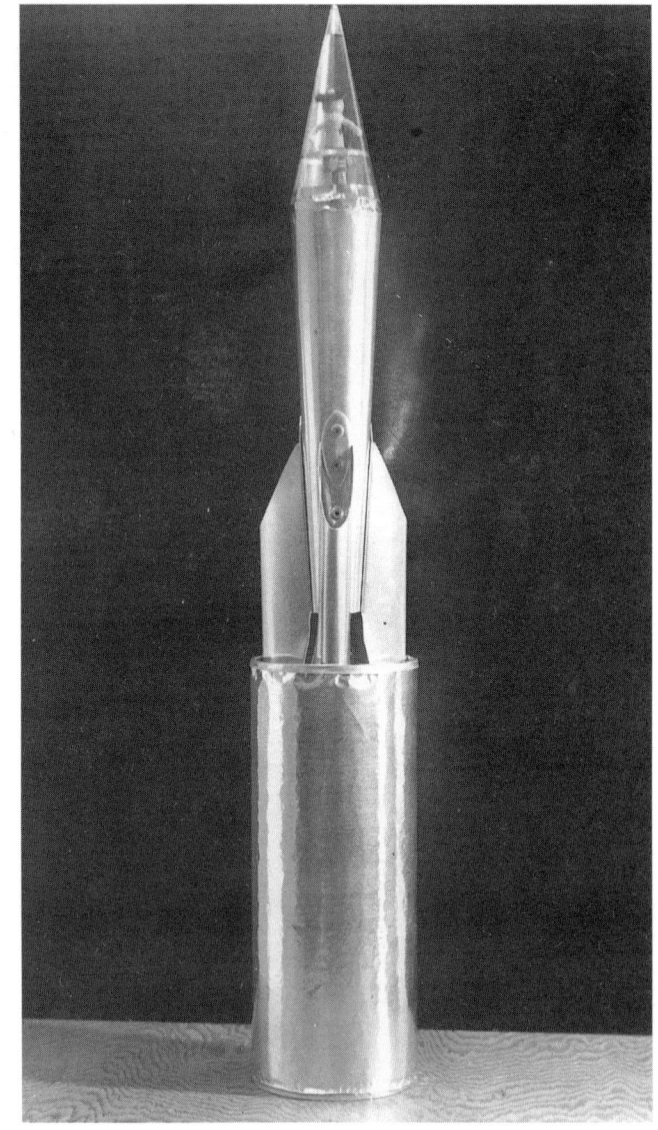

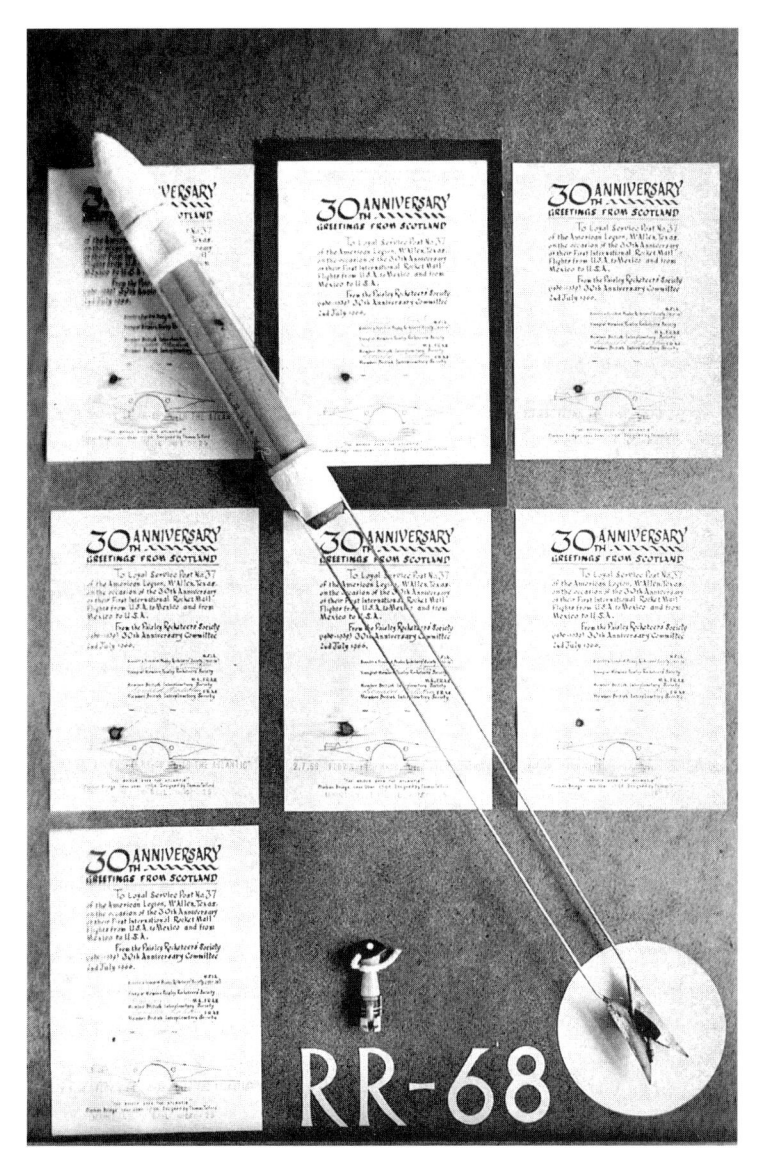

RR-68, the first of three rockets flown 'over the Atlantic' at Clachan Bridge, with a selection of the greetings message sheets. Miniature highlander 'Luck Macscott' flew in the compartment at the front with the 'window', and was sent to Mrs Rumbel, whose husband had flown the 'First International Rocket Mail' over the Rio Grande from the USA to Mexico. The twenty-five greetings were on thin paper, bound around the body of the rocket, and the 'blowout' scorched a hole right through all copies, including the cartridge paper original.

Alexander Lochhead lifts RR-68 from its landing position at Clachan Bridge, 2 July 1966. RR-69 was then flown from here back across the water to land on top of the cliff opposite.

30th ANNIVERSARY
GREETINGS FROM SCOTLAND

To Loyal Service Post No. 37 of the American Legion, McAllen, Texas, on the occasion of the 30th Anniversary of their First International Rocket Mail Flights from U.S.A. to Mexico and from Mexico to U.S.A.

From the Paisley Rocketeers' Society (1936-1939) 30th Anniversary Committee 2nd July 1966.

John R Stewart M.S.I.A.
Founder & President, Paisley Rocketeers' Society (1936-39)
Peter J Lumm
Youngest Member, Paisley Rocketeers' Society
Margaret S Watson M.A., F.R.A.S.
Member British Interplanetary Society
Donald Malcolm F.R.A.S.
Member British Interplanetary Society

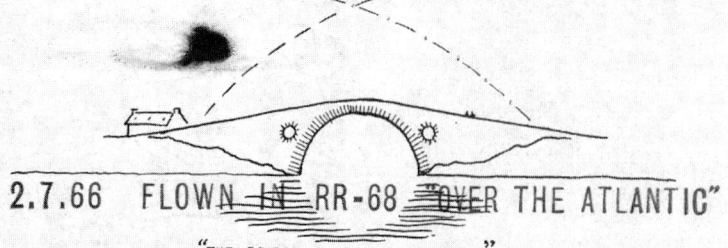

2.7.66 FLOWN IN RR-68 "OVER THE ATLANTIC"
"THE BRIDGE OVER THE ATLANTIC"
Clachan Bridge, near Oban 1792. Designed by Thomas Telford
MAINLAND TO SEIL No 18 OF 25

One of the greeting messages which was more seriously burnt by the 'blowout' from the motor.

An early aquajet, A-4, making its successful flight 'over the Atlantic' at Clachan Bridge, 31 August 1967. Twenty covers cacheted 'Seil-Mainland' were flown, while another twenty were marked 'Mainland-Seil'. The acetate tube forming the body of the aquajet had a slight curve, and it was necessary to spin the model by slightly angling the ends of the fins.

FLOWN "OVER THE ATLANTIC"
RR-78 TO SEIL ISLAND

ROCKET MAIL

26 OF 40

OBAN 4.45 PM 21 AU 67 ARGYLL

PAISLEY ROCKETEERS
15, BUSHES AVENUE,
PAISLEY, SCOTLAND
RECOVERED FROM SEA BY Colin MacQueen.
and Grahame MacQueen of Clachan

One of the ten covers ejected from the front of RR-78 when a blow-out from the rocket tube (motor) caused the rocket to swing around over the sea at Clachan Bridge. Nine of the covers were 'rescued' by the MacQueen brothers in their rowing boat.

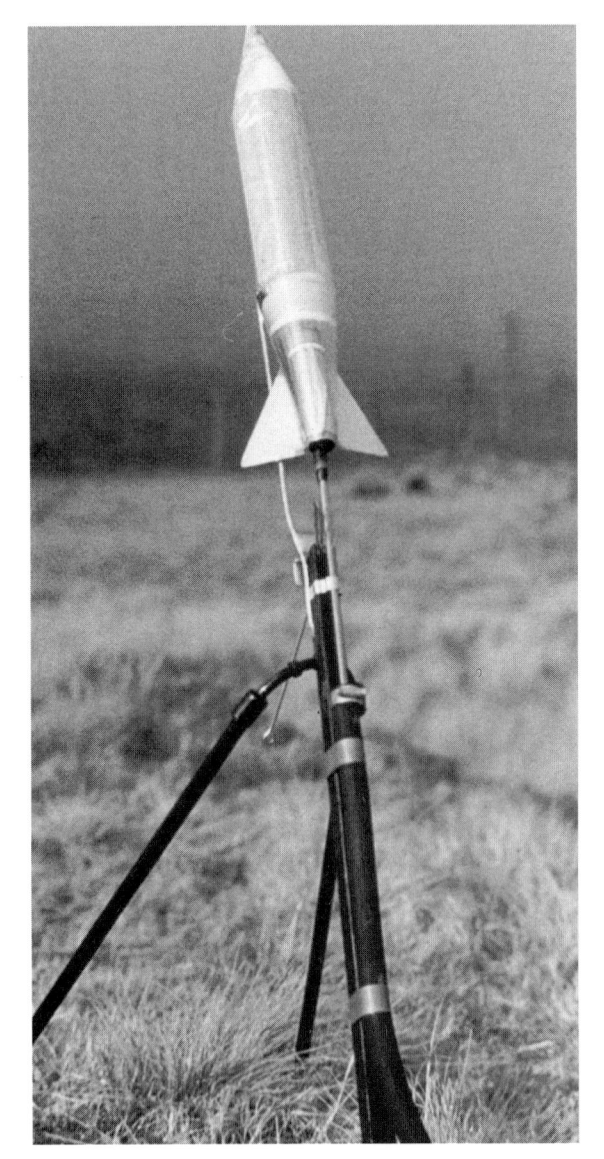

Since their reconstitution in February 1968, the Rocketeers have regularly organised charity fund-raising projects. This cover, from the second load launched to raise money for the 1968 Hurricane Relief Fund, was slightly damaged by water which leaked through the polythene wrapping.

A-15 in launching rack No. 2, April 11 1968. The aquajet is not properly fitted on the rack, but support rail is seen which can be folded back out of the way if not required. Vessels with short necks require support when launched at an angle.

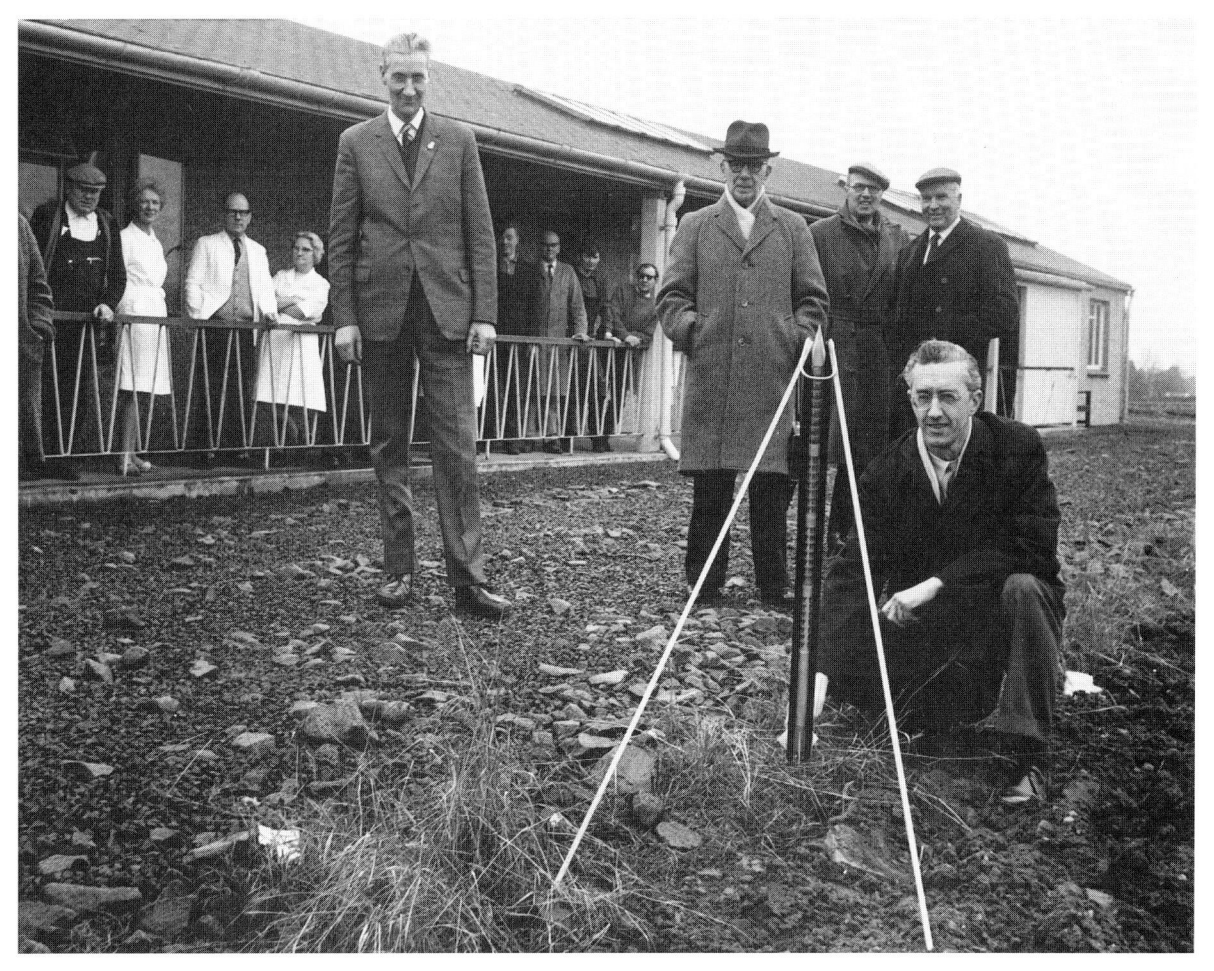

John Stewart prepares RR-85 for launch at the Linburn workshops of the Scottish National Institution for the War Blinded. Behind him are left to right: Peter Stewart; John R. Lockie; John Robertson; and A.G. Vallance MBE TD, Superintendent. This was the first launch of 'Paisley Pattern' charity rocket mail, and brought the Institution valuable publicity. The launch appeared on both BBC and ITV news that evening, 25 March 1969, and also brought a troublesome enquiry from the Home Office (Explosives Branch). The rocket was flown towards large, ploughed fields, within the grounds of the Institution, travelled a distance of about 1500 feet, and fell through the branches of a large tree. 100 covers were flown and cancelled first day of issue of the Concorde 4d stamp.

```
               EXPLOSIVES   BRANCH
                   HOME OFFICE
             Horseferry House, Dean Ryle Street, LONDON S.W.1
                  Telephone: 01-834-6655, ext.
                        Telex: 24986
Our reference:
Your reference:                    27 August 1969
```

Dear Sir,

Thank you for your letter of 31st July. After some consideration, I felt that I ought to write again, as I want to be quite sure that I have made the position clear.

I cannot alter my opinion that putting rocket tubes into model rockets is a source of danger, and in addition, I take the view that assembling the rocket tube to the rocket is an act of "manufacture", and as such is specifically prohibited by Section 4 of the Explosives Act 1875, unless in a factory licensed for the purpose by the Secretary of State.

We have always regarded fuelling a rocket by any means "manufacture" in this sense, and therefore illegal unless licensed: thus the same objections would apply to your fuelling the rockets in other ways, now that the use of the rocket tubes has been discontinued.

Thank you for your information about the source of supply of the rocket tubes.

                        Yours faithfully,

                        (J.G.N. POYNTZ)
                        H.M. Inspector of Explosives

John D. Stewart, Esq.
15 Bushes Avenue
Paisley
Renfrewshire
Scotland

A 'flimsy' designed by John Stewart depicting the Command Module and Lunar Excursion Module in orbit around the moon.

Under the headline ROCKETEERS "GROUNDED" BY HOME OFFICE. *Shock ban halts plans for national flying contest*, the Paisley Daily Express of 6/10/69 reported that: 'Paisley Rocketeers – who raise money for charity by flying "rocket mail" – have received an out-of-the-blue ban on their activities.' . . . 'The society, founded in 1936, has now been instructed by the Home Office in London: "No more rocket-flying." And the ban means that plans to have the first-ever National Rocket Flying Contest at Paisley have had to be scrapped by the local Rocketeers who were to play host to enthusiasts from throughout Britain at the event.'

When a researcher for the Dave Allen TV team spotted a PRS exhibit at the Museum of Childhood in Edinburgh, the society was asked to give a demonstration of aquajets, and staged the 3rd Aquajet Contest on 12 June 1976 when the team visited Paisley. Everyone in the photograph is looking very serious because this was the first launch and no one knew how the demonstration would go. Everything went very well, however, and there was much laughing and joking as the filming proceeded. The technicians started considering how they could make a launcher for their own children. Left to right: Jennifer Richmond; Neil Dryburgh; Alister Menzies; John Stewart; Gillian Richmond; Martin Macpherson; John Dryburgh and Dave Allen. The model is A-37/H, which launched a capsule of mail into the distance, then descended by streamers.

RR-97 on its faultless journey from Rudhaban Point to the Isle of Bute. The rocket landed neatly on the beach opposite. Had it dropped into the sea it would have floated with the tail sticking out of the water – to be recovered by Mr Colin Tebbut of Tighnabruaich in his dinghy.

John Stewart placing RR-100 in the launch rack near the top of Wells Hill. The rocket carried 100 covers, and after the flight they were printed to commemorate the 100th anniversary of Tsiolkovsky's 1883 theory that rockets could be used to propel vehicles through space. The launch was on 11 September 1983.

SPACEPROBE GIOTTO MEETS HALLEY'S COMET

Skyline ROCKETMAIL

13.3.86

FLOWN IN 6 SHOTS
A Q U A J E T 69
19.8.85 - 27.9.85
NO. 1 OF 50

PAISLEY ROCKETEERS' SOCIETY
15, BUSHES AVENUE
PAISLEY, SCOTLAND

Actual buildings of the Paisley skyline are depicted on this cover, with names and date of completion overleaf.

To commemorate the twentieth anniversary of our World's First Aquajet Contest of 1970, a contest between members was arranged for 16 September 1990 at Brodie Park. Permission to use the fenced off pitch and putt area as landing site was granted by Renfrew District Council. To reduce the range and make the results more visible to onlookers – as the public had been invited – launching was uphill. Left to right: John Bonsor, Graham Vassie, Graham E. Hill and Robert Law. John Bonsor acted as measurer and judge. He founded STAAR Research in 1989, and is its secretary (Space Technology Applications Astronomy & Rocket Research). Graham Vassie (and his brother Richard) produced some winning models. Graham E. Hill brought his model all the way from Rochester (Medway Rocket Group). Robert Law is wearing rocket enthusiast gear he brought back from a visit to Orlando, Florida.